DSLR

Photoshop Handbook & Dslr Photography Made

Easy

(A Beginner's Guide to Surviving Digital Slr

Photography)

Thomas Fowler

Published By Thomas Fowler

Thomas Fowler

DSLR: Photoshop Handbook & Dslr Photography Made Easy

(A Beginner's Guide to Surviving Digital Slr Photography)

ISBN 978-1-77485-409-9

Legal & Disclaimer

The information contained in this book is not designed to replace or take the place of any form of medicine or professional medical advice. The information in this book has been provided for educational and entertainment purposes only.

Author from and against any damages, costs, and expenses, including any legal fees potentially resulting from the application of any of the information provided by this guide. This disclaimer applies to any damages or injury caused by the use and application, whether directly or indirectly, of any advice or information presented, whether for breach of contract, tort, negligence, personal injury, criminal intent, or under any other cause of action.

You agree to accept all risks of using the information presented inside this book. You need to consult a professional medical practitioner in order to ensure you are both able and healthy enough to participate in this program.

TABLE OF CONTENTS

Introduction

Nowadays, the majority of photographers have shifted to DSLR photography. They've discovered that through DSLR photography, they can take excellent quality images. Photographers have discovered the many possibilities of DSLR photography since it can be used during the day , and in the evening.

If you are taking pictures of moving objects like racing vehicles, horses or bicycles, DSLR photography gives good images, and the feeling of motion is always captured in these images. DSLR cameras can also be used to capture environments of various landscapes and with the ability to adjust the settings, the pictures are good. This is the reason why it is increasing in recognition in the world of today. It's also fantastic for photographing moving water and water, which will always appear dreamy.

DSLR cameras come with several features that other cameras lack. While they're costly they are also fast, efficient and quality are not comparable with other cameras. They come with a variety of components that, when combined with their activities produce excellent photos. The cameras come with a variety of settings, and each one is designed to be used in specific and particular situations.

Chapter 1: Photography Basics

How to hold a camera

Let's start with the most fundamental aspect of photography, which is holding cameras. Many think that they have the ability to hold their camera, however I'll tell you that most beginner photographers make the wrong mistake. Don't fall for the temptation to overlook this part. It will form the foundation of your digital photography.

One of the most common issues with improper camera positioning is camera shake, which can be seen in a lot of amateur photographs. The blurring effect of images is evident. Camera shake happens when the camera isn't still when shutter is opened which causes that slight shake that has a negative impact on the quality the photo. If you are looking to make an occupation in photography or want to shoot excellent images, this is one thing to be aware of. Any slight movement in the camera can alter the picture. In dim lighting the problem gets worse because the shutter will open for a longer time. To stop this shake in your camera There are a variety of options you can take.

The most effective and preferred alternative is using tripod stands to keep your camera at a stable place. Tripod stands are made up of three legs, which ensure that the camera won't shake in any way. The majority of professional photographers utilize a tripod stand because they are aware of how beneficial it is for maintaining stillness that our hands cannot always accomplish. But it isn't always readily available, and in there are times when and you aren't able to put an appropriate tripod stand. In these scenarios, you need to make use of your hands, therefore we will explore how to hold your camera using your hands to take the most beautiful images.

One thing to keep in mind when using hands for holding the camera, is that we must avoid forming with one hand. Try as hard as you can using hands for holding the camera when you are focusing on the goal. This not only increases the stability, but also ensures that you are focusing correctly. The pattern of gripping will naturally depend on the camera you're using. Things like the where the lens is located, shutter size, the size of the camera and other factors will affect the way you hold the camera. There are however some guidelines that are applicable regardless of the camera that you're using. These are guidelines intended to assist a photography novice. They're not difficult and quick guidelines.

The first step is to use the left thumb to grip the left hand part on the camera. The forefinger must rest on the top of the shutter release. The thumb should be positioned to hold the camera's back and the rest of the fingers should be positioned around the front of the camera.

This will ensure you have the camera securely secured. Be sure to grip the camera in a manner that is strong enough however, not so tight that you shake. It is likely that modern cameras come with impressions that indicate where to place your fingers. This is very helpful, especially for those who are new to photography.

The left hand must hold the camera's weight since we've already seen that the right hand is meant to guide the location and stability that the camera is in. The left hand is best placed under the camera to help support the weight and ensure that the camera does not shake or tilt to the other side. If the camera is equipped with an optical lens or DSLR and the left hand could be placed underneath it to provide support.

Another tip for using your hands to stabilize your camera, is to fold into your elbows those sides to provide support. This will improve your stability in instances where you must focus for a longer duration of time.

Leaning against a thing that's sold like a wall or trees can improve your stability, and thus the stability the camera.

Therefore, if you have something you can lean on the more advantageous. If you don't then you could kneel or lie down. If you have to stand, place your feet at a distance of about a foot for additional stability. Keep in mind that for the camera to be in a still position the body needs to remain still. Relax and do what you can to improve your stabilization. For those who are just beginning, practice is the most effective method of getting your camera to hold properly. Do it slowly as you don't want your great photo to be damaged by camera shake. Once you master this technique, it will be ingrained in you and you'll forget about it, but in the beginning you must work hard to master it. Make sure to breathe slowly before you take the shot, as it aids in a state of calm.

Shutter Release

Shutter release is an additional important aspect to be discussed for novice photographers. It has a direct impact on the overall quality and clarity of photographs. Most beginners make this wrong and end up taking poor quality photos, and also miss out the best opportunities to capture photos quickly.

The benefit of the digital camera in comparison to film camera is they allow you to play as often as you like without cost.

The first thing to remember is that you must focus on applying a light pressure on the shutter, not hitting it. It's the same process employed when shooting with guns, where you slow press the trigger. This way, you can maintain the camera's stillness and also allow more control over the camera.

Second, when you press the shutter, don't use the point of the finger like beginners tend to do. Instead, utilize the flat portion of the first forefinger. This helps with improving control and maintaining a calm.

Chapter 2: ISO Setting

A way to think of it in terms of the dimensions of your garden or that of the bench you sit on. The ISO setting decides the number of plants or bushes you are able to plant. Also, how many people are able to be seated in the benches. Now you know the amount of light you can see in the photo for the spot in the sensor. This is how you select the camera's film. In the case of digital cameras, it will tell our how sensitive the camera is.

Then, this ISO value is constant, meaning that you cannot change it. Change only the other variables like time of the shutter and size. It is the ISO value is indicated by the f-stop number. Films will be able to record a certain amount of light for an ISO value, such as 100 (Dave Johnson January , 2006). If you increase the ISO value to 200, for instance and the sensitivity increases by two. The amount of light now increased by a factor of two. This makes your image more vibrant. Also, you will see many more trees for your backyard.

The issue with increasing this ISO setting is when you reach high values as the image begins to appear noisy. This isn't what you want to light because it can make the picture appear blurred. Imagine this as an excessive number of trees you don't need. To ensure that noise is kept out of your picture You should not go over 400. If you want to go over attempt 800. This is known as the film speed. Do not confuse it to shutter speeds.

Mechanism that is related to speed of film

You can adjust your shutter's speed either be either slow or fast. When the shutter speed is low, the amount of light that is captured by the film (or digital sensor) is greater. It is evident that in the reverse case, when shutter speed is high that the amount of light that can be absorbed into the camera will be lower.

From a film speed point of view from a speed perspective, you can pick the slow film or rapid film. A film with an ISO rating 200 is more efficient than one that has 100 ISO value. In this case, the relationship between light and speed is an inverse function of shutter speed. The slower film requires more light, while the faster film requires less light.

In terms of image quality the slow shutter gives an image with fine grain. The edges are well defined and we get more details in the tonal spectrum. In DSLR cameras there is less noise than when we choose an ultra-fast setting and a more ISO rating.

The ISO rating of a camera is used to determine the use of the camera.

Although this concept is more akin to film photography, you will see it listed on the DSLR camera. For example, it could include ISO 64 or ISO 800. The most expensive and large cameras will feature ISO 1600 or higher. Here's how to utilize the ISO value to maximize the performance the performance of you DSLR camera.

* If shooting outdoors in sunny conditions, use ISO 100 or ISO 200.

* If the light is diminishing such as in the evening hours or when skies are cloudy, choose ISO 400 or ISO 800.

* For filming at night, use ISO 1600. Yes, you should utilize a tripod as there is a high chance of motion.

Check the choices

Imagine you wanted to shoot exhibits in a dark space. Make sure you select ISO 1600, otherwise the sensors of the camera won't be able to detect light and you'll get an image that is dark. Another option is to use the flash to provide the required lighting. However, you'll be glaring and your backdrop for the photo is not lit effectively.

Modify the ISO settings

Click to activate the ISO button. After that, drag the buttons of navigation to the left/right or higher/lower positions to reach the position you need to be in. Alternately, you can select the auto position where the camera chooses the most appropriate position for that scene.

Scene in which you have to select the highest ISO value

Lower ISO values can give you images with an aesthetic balance and less grains. However, this number indicates which amount of light digital sensor can absorb. This is where we can find the instances where you need to use a more ISO to capture your image.

1. Use a tripod to lower the shutter speed

2. The object you are photographing is moving, and you need to "freeze" the action

3. The aperture is smaller to gain more depth of field

4. There are places in which you

want

to add grain to the image

5. If the light is evenly distributed and even to the subject as well as the background of the photograph.

If you're doing the actual photography, don't go to what you can see on the camera's visual display. The tiny optical display will display only the basic capabilities. Zooming in or out one time or twice, you'll be able to see the changes in brightness and color.

Other scenes that need a higher ISO

If you anticipate motion from the subjects in your shot You can select the higher ISO number for the camera. Because these are an image that is noisy make sure you select the appropriate shutter speed and aperture. For example:

1.Birthday celebrations, get-togethers, and gatherings

2. Church activities

3. Art Galleries and Exhibitions

4. Concerts

5. Sports events

If the event is held in a cloudy day or indoors the lighting will be lower than usual. In this case, the indoor lighting inadequate to allow normal ISO setting. There are also restrictions on for flash lighting, which can be seen in concert venues or churches as well as galleries and museums. The same issue is encountered when taking pictures of sporting events, however the issue is to freeze the image. In this case, too much movement and less light can result in dark and dull photos. Make sure to use ISO 1600 or higher depending on how dark your image is.

Size of the sensor and noise

One thing to take into consideration is how DSLR camera's full-frame image doesn't show any noise even at the highest ISO settings. However, there are many examples where a sensor that is small is not producing the expected noise. Also the size of the sensor follows the opposite relationship to noise. In other words, the less sensitive the sensors, the greater the noise. It's not always however.

Chapter 3: Camera Basics

When it comes to photography, it's crucial to be aware of the essentials. You must be equipped with the appropriate camera for your requirements. In addition, you need to know how to set the correct settings in your camera to ensure the most effective results you'd like for your photography.

Make sure you know your camera

Cameras are the main factor that determines your photography skills. First of all it's the main equipment you'll employ when you're on the "field" making photos. Without a camera, you'll not be able to accomplish anything. So, it's crucial that you understand your camera very well and also become friends with it.

But, even if you would like to take a leap to become the next big thing in photography, you're still not very comfortable in working with your most trusted photographer, your camera. You're still not sure about what the buttons and window do, and what you can do with the buttons. This is why below are the most fundamental components of digital cameras (these are based on popular camera that is not a DSLR):

A. shutter release. This button is utilized to take a picture and controlling the exposure of your image and focus. If you press this button half-way and you are able to secure the focus and exposure of your photo. If you press it to the fullest it will be able capture the image.

b. Control buttons. These buttons can be used to turn up or down the focus feature as well as the automatic flash or other functions of your camera. They can also be used to adjust the image's quality and to turn on the self-timer (which is extremely useful for photographers and want to be included in the photograph).

C. Dial for setting the shooting mode. This button is used for setting the mode of shooting which is why it's called "shooting dial." You can select from a variety of shooting modes offered by your camera, including Night Mode, Portrait Mode, Landscape Mode, and other modes, based on the subject you wish to capture.

d. Microphone. This is crucial when recording video and audio footage (of course, you would not utilize this for taking photos). Sometimes, this may trigger the self-timer, which is activated by sounds.

The e. the Focus Light Aid. This is the source of the auxiliary illumination that allows the camera have greater concentrate on what you're taking pictures even though the lighting is dim.

The f. Electronic Flash. It is used to give enough light to shoot your photos in dim lighting. It also helps to fill with shadows that are dark.

G. optical viewfinder. This window is utilized to frame your photos and also for creating your photographs.

H. Zoom lens. It is utilized for zooming in and out, when you need to magnify something or snap photos of things that are quite from your.

i. Lens cover. It protects lenses of cameras while it's not using it.

j. Tripod socket. This is which connects the tripod, which then assists your camera.

k. Docking/USB port. This port connects the camera with your PC in order to transfer files. In certain cameras it is also utilized to charge the battery.

L. The battery compartment. This is where the battery is placed.

M. The power switch. This is obviously the switch that allows you to switch your camera off or on.

n. Indicator LEDs. These LEDs indicate that you're in the right focus and exposure. They typically either green or red.

o. Display the control/menu button. It is the place where you can control the information that appears in your display. It is also where you're taken to different menus that are available in your camera, like the setup menu, record menu as well as other menus and features of the camera.

P. Preview of the photo. This button lets you preview your pictures you've already taken.

Q. The Cursor button. This button allows you to navigate through the options in the camera's menu. There are other cameras with buttons that can additionally be utilized to gain access important functions of the camera, like the macro mode, flash as well as the exposure level.

r. Set/execute button. This is the button you use to enable a particular feature you've selected in the drop-down menu (otherwise called"OK" button).

s. Memory slot for cards. This slot is used to store your memory card, which will add more memory to your camera.

t. File-save LED. This light signifies that an photo is currently being stored or loaded onto you memory card.

Formats for files

Images captured by your camera and later loaded onto your drive will have different file formats. Of course, all the files to be saved (documents or videos, audios, etc.) are saved in file formats.

For photographers It is equally important that you know the basics in terms of the formats of your files as it can also affect the final photo you'll receive in the future.

a. Tagged Image File Format (TIFF). TIFF files are thought of as to be the "industry standards for digital photos" in accordance with Langford's Basic Photography. They can be easily compressed or uncompressed using your personal computer, as well editing them using any editing software you like.

b. RAW. RAW files are "raw" or uncompressed files directly from the camera's memory. That's why you have the name RAW. Since they are raw, it is dependent on your preference whether you wish to have your files compressed or not compressed. Additionally than that, these files can be edited using the favorite photo editing software. When it comes to size, RAW files are about 1/3 smaller than TIFF files. Therefore, you will be able to store more RAW files in the memory of your computer than you can with TIFF.

C. Joint Photographic Experts Group

(JPEG). It is the most widely used file format that is used when it comes to images. In fact, Langford declared JPEG images as an "undisputed top-of-the-line file formats." Contrary to TIFF or RAW files, however, JPEG are already compressed files, however it doesn't necessarily suffer a significant reduction in quality when compared to other formats for files. Because it's compressed and compressed, it is a JPEG file is only one-tenth of the size of an TIFF file, which means you will be able to store more JPEG images within your devices.

Optical zoom vs. Digital zoom

If you're not into photography in general then you can simply refer to zoom the same thing as "zoom. You'll no need to be thinking about whether it's an optical or digital zoom. You are however working towards being a professional photographer therefore it is crucial to recognize the distinction between the two. Both are features that all cameras with no SLR feature.

According to Langford Here's the main distinction between the two:

a. Optical zoom. This type of zooming utilizes the arrangement of lenses to adjust the magnification. This is typically the first choice among the options available to you on your camera.

b. Digital zoom. This zooming option is an additional feature which enlarges the central pixels of your image using a mathematical algorithms. This allows you to fill all the space of your photograph with the data contained in the center pixels.

Aperture, shutter speed and ISO

In photography, there are the so-called jargonsthat only those with at the very least an understanding of photography can be able to comprehend. These terms include an aperture and shutter speed as well as ISO rating.

a. Aperture. Based on Julie Adair King, author of Shoot Like a Pro: Digital Photography Techniques, aperture is the "iris inside the lens" which can be adjusted based to the light entering through the lens of the camera. The aperture's size is indicated by "f-numbers which are written using the letter f at the beginning after that a dash, then the number (e.g. f/2.8). The f-number as well as the aperture size are in inverse relation which means that If you set the f number larger, your aperture will be smaller and reverse.

B. Speed of shutter. King also described shutter as an "window shade" behind the lens of the camera. When you take a picture it opens the shutter for a short time to allow light to pass through the lens, and then get to the image sensor inside the camera. The speed of shutter, on the other hand, refers to the length of time the duration that the shutter is open.

If the shutter's speed remains low (which means that the shutter stays open for longer) and more light will be able to enter the lens of the camera.

C. ISO rating. ISO rating in contrast, is used to indicate the sensitivity of light required by the camera's image sensor. If you make an ISO number higher it will be more light sensitivities.

Exposure Modes

Many digital cameras, regardless of whether a point-and shoot camera or an SLR camera, have the programmatic auto-exposure (AE). If you're in the programed

AE mode, the camera will automatically determine the optimal combination of aperture and shutter speed required to give you the best exposure.

In addition to the programmed AE however, some sophisticated computers allows for more variations on the subject: aperture-priority AE, which permits your camera to determine the shutter speed after you've set the aperture. There is also the shutter priority AE, which permits the camera to set the aperture when you've determined the shutter speed.

But, your camera might also let you alter the aperture manually and shutter speed based on your preferences.

Chapter 4: Technology

1.Megapixel - Truth vs. Fiction

Pixels are the basic components of a digital camera. Each pixel is an image-diode. The Photo-diode collects light transforms the light into RAW digital signal. Each photo-diode connects to the unit that processes images through an electrical wiring network which transmits the electronic signals to the processing unit to be processed further. Pixels directly affect the resolution and size of an sensor. More pixels, the higher resolution. One million pixels equals one megapixel.

Pixels are generally similar in size to dots. However, there is an occasional difference. For the sake of argument, let's say that a pixel is essentially one printed dot. It is easy to identify the optimal resolution for printing a particular size photo. The industry standard for printing of 300dpi. For an image that is print-quality for example, 4" 6" it only requires an 2.16 resolution! It's 4 x300 6 x 600 x 300 1,000,000 is 2.16. If you only would like to display an image on an HD TV with an resolution of 1080 x 1920 pixels pixels, you only need an 2.07 millimeter sensor!

This means that all suddenly all the talk about higher resolution. doesn't seem to be relevant any more, doesn't it?

2.RAW 3.RAW. JPEG

The RAW contrasts with JPEG debate is likely to be the second most heatedly discussed one, following the Nikon debate. Canon debate. It is true that RAW is an uncompressed format and not processed. It means that you will get a basic synthesis of information that you can work on and then give a final glance at. RAW is a raw 12-bit file that contains all of the data that was gathered by the camera during the exposure. The possibilities are endless. JPEG is, however, a different matter. JPEG is a lost and processed file. It is already being modified using the built-in software of the camera. The colors are more vibrant and the image is more sharp and the white balance is already in place in accordance with the settings you have selected. A raw file that has not been processed RAW file On the other hand is flat and visible less sharp.

3.Image stabilization Do you think it is important?

In one word it's yes! Images Stabilization (IS) can be described as an optical innovation and is a feature that was added to cameras later. Image stabilization lets photographers utilize slower shutter speeds while using a hand to hold the camera. It also lets him make use of a long focal length without needing tripod. Image Stabilization has gone through a series of changes over time. When it first was introduced, manufacturers had a split over what was the most effective method to introduce image Stabilization on cameras. Should it be put on the camera's body?

Should it be put in front of the lens? The skills of design and marketing can lead to progress within both directions.

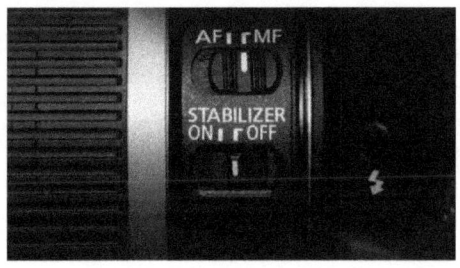

These two technologies are widely used. Sony's body-based image stabilization technology makes all their lenses automatically stabilized. On the other hand Nikon and Canon who are supporters of the lens-based image stabilization technology, have produced numerous lenses that have built-in image stabilization features. They do not rely on the current technology and that means that older cameras equipped with an appropriate mount can benefit from the stabilization function of images.

Okay, so that's an overall concept of the various types that image stability. But does IS matter? Let's consider an instance. Let's say that you're shooting photographs of sunset portraits with your hands on the camera. The meter tells you that the proper exposure for ISO 200 is f/4 and shutter speed of 1/60 second. It is 85mm focal length. Every time you take the picture and then look at it you find that the pictures aren't sharp. Are you wondering why this happens? It's because when you choose shutter speeds that are greater than the opposite that of your focal length you're automatically at risk of shake in your image.

The general rule is to utilize a higher shutter speed, which is in this instance at minimum 1/100 of a second. At 1/100, however, your images will be underexposed. This is the point where image stabilization enters the picture in the literal sense. Image stabilization is a way to compensate for non-intentional hand movements and allows the photographer to take pictures at slower shutter speed than normally achievable. Based on the technology, it can be up to two or three stops faster, which is an advantage particularly when shooting in dim light conditions like the ones previously mentioned.

Chapter 5: Exposure Triangle

1.Aperture 1. The Hole in the Box

Rotate the camera to face you. The shutter button is pressed. Did you notice that a gap was created for a brief period, then it shut as it resets the shutter? This hole is known as the aperture. It allows light to enter when you push on the button to release the shutter. The diameter of the hole can be controlled by a sequence of blades called diaphragms. The blades are moved according to the aperture you set to create the hole.

Aperture Range

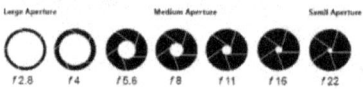

Light that comes through an aperture will be directed to the sensor in the rear of the camera (or film, in the case might be) making it visible and recording an image. Aperture is a crucial part of the holy three-part equation of exposure. The other two components are shutter Speed as well as ISO.

Aperture is expressed as the form of f-stops. The exact size of the lens's opening (which is an exact measure of aperture) is determined by dividing your lens' focal length by the number of f-stops. For example, let's say you have 100mm prime lens adjusted to f/2.8. The lens's diameter will be 100/2.8 = 35.71

The aperture value or the f-stop number will provide you with an indication of what aperture you're using is large or small. F/2.8 is an aperture that is large. It will let in lots of light. In comparison, f/11 is a tiny aperture that allows only a tiny amounts of light. F/22 is much smaller. Small apertures are ideal to capture landscapes. An aperture that is larger is ideal for portraits and flower photography and subject separation from background and so on.

The aperture controls the the depth of field. Depth of field refers to the extent to which an image is in focus. If the majority part of an image appears blurred with the exception of the subject, it's described as having a low depth of field. If the majority of the image is sharp, it's an example of high deep field. As discussed in the previous paragraph, both large and shallow depths of field come with specific uses in photography.

2.Shutter Tempo & Speed = Creativity the exposure

Shutter speed is the length of time that the shutter remalns open, and the sensor that is behind is open to light. Naturally, the that the longer shutter stays open, more sunlight that's captured. This is among the numerous shooting modes that are marked on the dial for mode. On Nikon systems, the Shutter Priority mode is identified with the letter "S". On Canon systems, it is labeled as "Tv" which stands for Time Value. Shutter speed is calculated in fractions of a second such as 1/100, 1/200 and so on. The smaller the fraction, the more rapid the shutter speed. Shutter speeds of one second or more (slower) are measured in 1" 2" and then on. Shutter speed is among the three components that comprise the triangle of exposure. The two other elements are Aperture Valuation and ISO.

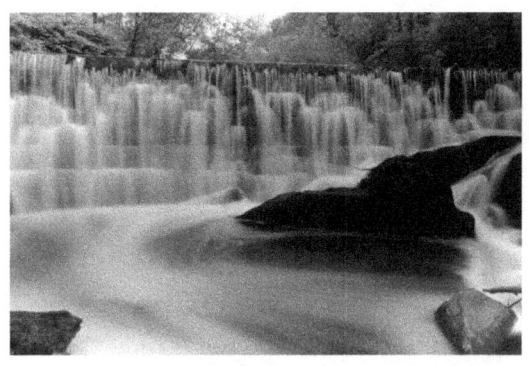

There are numerous inventive uses for shutter priority modes. Longer shutter speeds are utilized to capture motion blur, giving those captivating light trails as well as long star trails blurred ocean and cityscapes against a lake in the night. Long exposures are also the most popular method of shooting fireworks as well as light painting. It is also a great method for taking pictures of waterfalls in bright sunlight. There are a few ancillary equipment that are required to shoot long exposures in bright lighting. We will discuss those in a future post.

3.ISO Sensor Sensitivity and Noise explained

The digital sensor in the DSLR camera is at the center of. The sensor's digital sensors capture light, and converts to electronic signal that are processed further and stored in JPEG or JPEG or unprocessed RAW in the event that it is. ISO Settings are expressed as numbers. The greater the number, the more responsive the image is likely to be.

However, this increased sensitiveness comes at a cost and that price is noise. Noise is caused by the fact that at higher sensitivity , sensors attempt to amplify the signals. Because light signals are weak the sensor will produce an abundance of noise. This is similar to the noise in audio or TV signals, when amplified.

In the early days of film photography, photographers had confront grain. While not exactly the same thing, noise is often described in the same way by the name film grain.

Another reason that noise can occur is due to the higher resolutions of sensors. A higher number of megapixels is not good as long as you consider that the dimensions of the chip is the same. Cameras with smaller sensors. The smaller Point & Shoot camera comes with an area of 1/2.3" when compared to the full-frame 36x24mm sensor on a camera, such as that of the Nikon D800. A smaller sensor chip and more pixels it contains and smaller the size of each pixels. When the pixels begin to shrink, they are prone to light leakage which causes noise.

4.Exposing right

This technique is often employed when a photographer isn't able to determine the proper exposure for a particular scene. This technique , and occasionally the method that is known as Auto Exposure Bracketing (AEB) can be used to solve the issue. AEB is used most often for creating High Dynamic Range (HDR) images. Exposed to the left refers to setting a setting where the exposure meter shows it is tilted towards an upward direction (over-exposure). This is done to in order to get a little more clarity from shadow areas. The idea behind this is that you can always decrease the amount of light that is reflected in certain parts of the image by with the burn tool available in Photoshop. If you do try to increase the brightness (using the burn tool) you'll likely create noise.

Chapter 6: Lighting

The lighting can affect the entire picture you capture. This is why the settings of the camera are so crucial as discussed in the previous section. They are however options to choose from and once you determine the ideal lighting to create the atmosphere of your photos you will be able to be more picky about the times to shoot. The ideal time of day is always when the lighting is ideal for the picture you'd like to get.

Outdoor lighting

It doesn't matter how the weather is going. You can take stunning and dramatic images outside even in the midst of dark and scary. Portraits that are shot outdoors, you should focus on the central subject and, if it's one person, concentrate upon the face. The f stop on your camera must be set to allow an extremely low depth of field (f2 or f/4) since these are focused on your main subject and the background is blue. Make sure you don't make use of a lens smaller than 50mm. Make adjustments to the camera to ensure that photos are saved as RAW files. The problem with the jpg. Files is that they are compressed, and they can be able to lose a lot of detail , especially when you are shooting outdoors. it is essential to the light and to the overall appearance of the photo.

Natural lighting outdoors

Always photograph with the sun in the background. Otherwise, the fine detail you could see in the viewfinder could be lost. It's best to apply this guideline for portraits. In the event that the sun's on the left, it could result in losing significant detail. If the sun is behind your subject, it can cause blurred vision. Check out the clarity of this girl's eyes. It's perfect. The lighting was amazing and, at f/2.8 with an ISO of 200 the image is excellent quality.

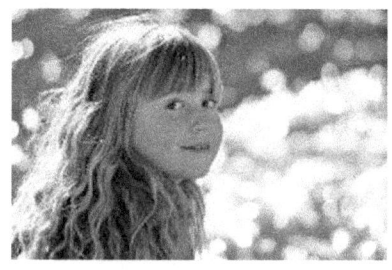

Indoor natural lighting

The natural light that comes from windows can add a dramatic look to the portrait. If you have the benefit of natural light, make use of it instead of adding flash because it will hinder the quality of your photo. Natural light can be very dramatic and can add drama to your photo. It also gives the appearance of softness. Check out the light that is natural in this photo to see a good illustration.

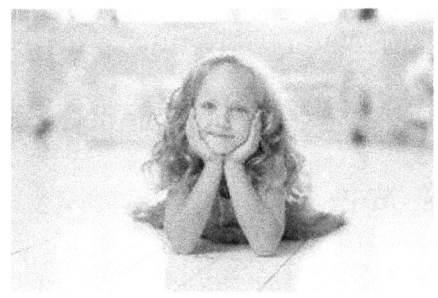

This image was shot with natural light. The camera used was an Canon 85.0mm with the shutter speed set at 1/122 sec on f/1.8 and the ISO at 200.

If you want to bring lighting into your indoor space You should consider using diffused light that is scattered into the area you require it. In studios, this is accomplished by using spotlights that bounce off silver or white parasols. It is possible to achieve the similar effect by using an umbrella made of white. Explore different angles for the face, too, as light reflections can reflect off the most desirable side of the face to give the image that has real dimension and personality.

Chapter 7: Discover to Control the Shutter Speed

Mechanism of shutter

For the uninitiated the shutter speed may not refer to anything. Because it is one of the essential aspects you need to control in order to take an excellent image It is crucial to know how it works. The shutter is located in the front of your lens. It closes and opens when you press the camera's photo button. The speed at the shutter opens and closes is known as the shutter speed.

The concept of speed

If the shutter speed is extremely high and the lens is open only for a fraction of one second. The amount of light released into the camera is minuscule. You should use a quick film when you are doing this. If you prefer using a slower film, then the shutter should be open for a longer time.

Low and high speed

In the case of a DSLR camera, it is possible to have the option to select shutter speeds that are fast like 1/8000 of second, or when the shutter speed is only for a few seconds. The camera may utilize abbreviated numbers like '500' to indicate the speed of 1/500.

Choose the shutter speed that is right for you.

It is only necessary to have a fast shutter speed only when you are taking action sequences with high speed, such as machine in motion. The movement that is not needed is cut and during the time that the camera is opened the action is frozen' (Nasim Mansurov, December 2009). One example is when you need to capture motion-laden scenes, like waterfalls. In this case, you should select an aperture that is low. The aim is to incorporate the motion into the image and show this as blur. This adds an attractive glow to the image. If you're taking photographs of the night sky You may keep your shutter unlocked for a few minutes. This will allow the digital sensor to take great pictures.

The dangers of shutter speeds that are low

Be aware that if you shoot at shutter speeds lower than 1/60, you'll get loud movement. To minimize this, utilize tripods. When taking hand-held photos you should lean against the wall or lie down on your back when you are using an aperture that is long or when shutter is not high. The camera should be placed against your face to ensure that shake is lessened when you press. Keep your elbows the vicinity of your body to rest and stabilize your arms to limit movements. In general any shutter speed that is greater than 60 500, 125 or 1250 is considered an extremely high shutter speed. Anything less than 60, such as 30 and 15 are slower values for shutter speeds.

Auto shutter speed and manual.

If you would like your camera to select the shutter speed that you prefer select the 'S' symbol to select the shutter. Most cameras will be images showing the position of the camera. They could show outside as well as incandescent, cloudy or incandescent. If your shutter is set for this image the camera will select the aperture to ensure that your image will be high-quality. This top shooting position comes with two options - Tv and Av positions. In the Tv position one set the shutter speed in advance. Camera will calculate the most suitable aperture for the particular scene and then use it.

Choose different positions

In the Av mode, you select the aperture first. This lets the camera choose the shutter speed that will allow the required light into the camera. If you want to go the manual method, select "M". You will need to select the aperture size that corresponds to your shutter speed. pick.

As we mentioned the focal length plays an important role in the option you choose. If it is divided by shutter speed then we will get what is known as the size of aperture. If you're not attentive when selecting the aperture correctly, you may experience camera shake. Make sure you adjust the aperture, and then select the smaller ISO value. This gives you flexibility in deciding to increase the speed of shutter.

Alternate the speed of shutter

This procedure is simple.

* Turn to the camera.

Find the dial for the position and set it to TV the position (or the Av position).

* Turn the dial for shutter speed to the required amount.

The most important thing to keep in mind to keep in mind is that the camera can require a couple of seconds to begin again if shutter speed is not high. Therefore, you need to be patient till the camera appears fully operational before taking the next shot. Click the shutter halfway until you see the orange light on the screen of the viewfinder.

Chapter 8: Digital Photography Gear for Beginners

The majority of beginners to photography are obsessed about the latest photography gear. They are looking for the most modern and efficient equipment. But when photography is involved the most recent technology isn't always the best choice for you, let alone the extra costs. Actually, you can get amazing photos with a basic camera. It's not just the camera that enhances its quality photos but the experience you get from the various settings available.

At first you'll need equipment to begin. A camera and lens are essential. You will need an tripod stand along with a bag, memory cards and an editing program. Other items like lighting could be purchased later. It is important to be patient before you make any purchase to ensure you only purchase the things you require. There is a tendency to be a beginner to buy the marketing hype and spend a lot of money on things only to find that you really didn't require the items you bought in the first place. As you gain experience, the more you learn about photography and you will be able to see the things you need and you are able to make purchases later on.

Cameras

On the market there are a myriad of cameras available that it can leave novice confused about which one to purchase. Each camera is advertised using different terms to confuse the buyer. One thing that marketers have used to their advantage is megapixels. They have made us believe that the higher the number of megapixels, the better, but that's not always the reality.

I would say that for beginners, most digital cameras available are suitable for you. The most important thing to consider for you right now is the price. Do not go into debt to purchase the highest priced camera. Make sure you buy what you can afford right now, and when you've gained the needed experience , you can make a decision to invest. Canon or Nikon are the most popular brands when it comes down to cameras. A few of the technical features to be looking for are ISO Sensitivity, which refers to the capacity of the camera to capture high-quality photos in dim light circumstances. A higher ISO is great for your camera. But keep in mind that your camera is required to create high-quality images with this high ISO. One aspect of technology that you should not even think about is the number of the number of megapixels. Although we hear about this often, it's reasonable to conclude that all digital cameras on the market today contain plenty of millimeters to capture high-quality images.

There are other things to think about prior to purchasing cameras. One of them is where you will take the photos or the purpose you intend to use the camera for as well as the battery time that the camera has is vital considering the majority of photography is outdoors, and power supply is a problem.

Lenses

Lenses are the second most important aspect of photography, after the camera. For beginner and experienced photographers, picking the right lens could be a nightmare. The quality of the lens you choose can greatly affect the overall quality and image of your images. I would suggest that beginners use the camera by itself and the lens by itself instead of buying the camera and lens that is part of the package. This gives you to have a wider choice of the lens you use according to your needs for photography. There are two kinds of lenses: the zoom lenses as well as the prime lenses. Zoom lenses, as their name suggests come with a zoom function.

Similar to cameras, canon and Nikon are the top two brands in the field of lenses too. There's not much of a an difference between these two firms in terms of quality. Beginners can select the 50mm lens category from these brands. They're perfect for beginners and cost-effective. Before deciding on the lens you want to use ensure whether it's compatible with your camera.

Storage devices

You need to invest in high-quality storage devices in order not to lose your most important photos. Memory cards and an external hard drives of top quality are crucial. Don't put your photos in DVDs and CDs since they be less durable. Today, we have cloud storage that is an excellent backup to all your favorite photos.

Tripod

Tripod stands are an absolute must for anyone who wants to take those stunning photographs. It is not necessary to pay for the most costly; there are plenty of excellent ones at fairly affordable costs.

Cleaning and maintaining the camera gear

Cameras and their accessories can be expensive. to extend their time of use, we have to maintain them regularly. As with everything else, with regular maintenance they'll last effectively and maintain the superior quality photos we would expect from them. This is not the case. Many people believe that they don't pay their cameras the respect they deserve, which causes high-cost losses for equipment and the quality of images. The reason is because they don't know how to maintain and clean their cameras. For those who are just beginning, it can be more difficult since they're just beginning to learn about photography, and are extremely enthusiastic and all they want is to snap pictures with their new camera. Make sure you periodically clean your camera equipment to ensure that they're in top shape. There is no cost to get these products. I'll show you how you can do them yourself without posing a risk to the environment. Like most things in living, preventing is more effective than solving problems, and so the majority of my advice is geared towards getting rid of any issue in the first place, rather than dealing with the aftermath of an issue later.

Humidity is your camera's and lenses' biggest enemy. The high humidity could easily harm our cameras if not cautious. If you reside in an area with high humidity or snap photos in such places you must be extra cautious. The camera's sensor is affected by humidity which can greatly impact the quality of photographs. Therefore, we must ensure that our cameras are completely dry. Get a sturdy camera bag that is well-padded to protect your camera when it is not being used. When using it, stay away from moving from cold areas to warm environments, such as in a room where your camera is in use.

Cleaning the camera

Different components within the camera have distinct cleaning needs. The lens, sensor mirror, outer casing and mirror will be cleaned in different ways. We will take a look at them individually and decide what and when you should clean them. A word of warning in this regard is to be cautious in cleaning all the areas from your cameras. If you're not certain about any of the items, put it aside rather than damage and incur a huge cost to repair or replace it. But, cleaning your home isn't an easy task.

The lens is the first thing to be considered as this is the most critical component of your camera. It requires a lot of attention when it comes to cleaning. Lenses are not easy to fix and any damage can force the purchase of a new lens. Careful when cleaning the lens. A fine tissue and an alcohol-solvent should be sufficient to cleanse the glass parts of the lens. The material must be of good quality and specially designed to be used for this task. A blower can help to eliminate dust particles from rear and front elements. The moving elements of the lenses must also be cleaned with the blower brush in order to keep the smoothness of motion.

The final component is the camera's sensor. This is the most delicate area of the camera.in fact , most people prefer to bring their camera to a professional cleaner in order to get rid of dust particles from the sensor. But, it is something you can accomplish on your on your own, but you must exercise extreme care. In the beginning, you must switch the camera into manual mode. (remember the settings we spoke about in the first chapter.) Make sure to set the exposure for 30 seconds to allow enough time to clean the sensor prior to when the shutter is closed. Make sure you don't use the bulb setting when the sensor remains open for longer, because the shutter could close due to other reasons such as power , creating damage. You not only damage the sensor, but it also damages the mirror as well as the shutter itself. The manual mode that has 30 seconds delay gives the time to clean, and allows you to set the time for your work to finish before the timer is done. It is possible to continue with another time when the shutter is closed with another delay set. Cleaning is fairly easy, just keep the camera facing downwards while the shutter is open and then blow it to remove dust particles.

Make sure you don't utilize the blower brush just the blower. The sensor could be filthy and greasy, and the blower does not do a lot cleaning. In this situation it is necessary to have cleaning alternatives that allow you to physical clean your sensor. This is a delicate process to handle and is only performed only when absolutely necessary.

Mirrors are the main part of the cleaning process. This isn't as delicate as the lens or sensor component and, in reality, does not affect the the final picture except to the point that it makes it impossible to see your subjects clearly. However, it could need to be cleaned regularly. and dust transfer onto other areas in the lens.

The final component of the camera we're going to take a look at is the casing's outer and accessories. They are just as important as the other components. External parts are able to transmit dirt to the interior. Make use of a blower brush to clean the dust off, afterwards, use a tissue to clean the area quickly. Begin by cleaning the outside of the components before moving on to the interior parts.

When storing your camera , make sure to use a sturdy, clean bag. Make sure you don't store your camera at high temperatures like in the trunk compartment of your car , or when temperatures are below freezing. Protect the lenses by caps to prevent any damage.

Chapter 9: Aperture

Do you recall in school a bit of debate about pupils of the eyes? The pupil of your eyes determines whether light is diffused or absorbed. The iris of your eye will expand as the pupil dilates or gets larger in dim light to ensure that more light can enter your eye. In the daylight, when the sun is shining your iris gets smaller and the pupil shrinks (gets smaller) due to the fact that less light has to pass through your pupil so that you can see.

If you can think about how your eyes work and how your eye works, you will be able to understand the way that aperture functions in your camera.

Terminology

The aperture is the opening in the lens.

What exactly is Aperture?

In camera terms, Iris and Aperture are generally interchangeable. The aperture determines the amount of light that can be reflected to the camera's sensor. When you alter the aperture settings on your camera, you're expanding or decreasing the size of the opening. This is usually called the diaphragm.

The Aperture value is displayed in your camera's F/stops. If you turned the Av dial just to play with the settings with it, you'll notice things such as f/2.8 or f/11. You also noted that you could alter the settings by reading f/4.0 or F/16.

DSLR cameras may have 1/3 or 2/3 of the full stop which means you can alter the aperture setting in thirds to produce more precise images. The lower numbers, like f/2.8 are more aperture settings. This means the opening is higher than an f/16 stop.

If you're shooting images in low lighting, you'll need something around f/2.8 This means that the shutter can be opened larger to let more light to enter. If you are getting plenty of light then you must reduce the aperture so that you can reduce the amount light coming into the camera.

Sizes and positions

The sizes and positions of apertures are dependent upon the focal. In certain DSLR cameras an aperture control mechanism sits located directly behind the lens. This means that an f/8.0 aperture setting on the 20mm wide-angle lens will be smaller than that of 300mm telephoto lens. However, f/8.0 aperture allows to let the exact amount of light to pass through to the sensor of the image in both lens.

Field Depth Field

Do you remember the setting that is related to the depth of field on the dial for mode? You should know that depth of field could be affected by the aperture settings you choose. A smaller depth of field can be found by letting more light or let the shutter open wider than you would with a narrower shutter. That means that when there is a less wide opening to let light in and more focus is focused on the front and background of the object, rather than the focus point.

When it comes to photography, the standard is to have a 1/3 depth of field to your subject's front and two-thirds of the focus to the backdrop of an object. In a photo the eyes are typically more on the subject in focus than on the surrounding regions, which is why you can make a more sharp flower image when you alter the f/stop so that the flowers come in focus, and also reduce both the foreground and background into blurred mess.

Photograph Example 6: Testing F/Stops an object stationary

Find something near you while reading this. It could be a plant or a cat sleeping or something else. If you're in a space that is dark however you have plenty of lighting, you can begin to take photos at every aperture setting. You may also alter the lighting conditions of the room you are in (if indoors) and begin testing every aperture setting.

Download the images, and then compare the two images to determine the difference that the size of the opening makes an impact on the subject. Some of them will display the object as blurry against the background or the foreground while others reverse the image.

Yes, the camera's focus can make a difference, However it is important to examine everything, you're making sure that your lens is focused and that you're using a tripod in order to keep the camera in place.

Photo Example 7: The Moon

Once you've mastered ISO and shutter speed and you've learned regarding apertures, we can head into the lunar sphere. According to experts, the aperture should be f/11. This is the ideal setting to begin with using manual modes. It is also possible to experiment with the setting to see if you are able to improve the quality of your images by using the other setting.

F/11 offers an aperture of 16 that could not be enough dependent on the moon's. The full moon will have plenty of direct sunlight to concentrate on, and a larger opening can impact the clarity or depth of field. You might need to raise the aperture to f/16 in order to ensure that the opening isn't as large to ensure that the camera doesn't overthink the problem.

The majority of photography is about trying various settings until you can get the result you desire. The practice of using your camera can help you to understand how it functions in various scenarios. What might work for one person could not be the photo you want to capture. Therefore, even though beginning by using ISO 200,

F11, and 1/125 may work for certain people who want to capture the moon's light, it could not work for the image you're hoping to capture.

Chapter 10: Understanding the Metering Modes and Focus Modes

Focus modes and metering modes are also little features that will enable you to have more control over your camera. You have access to your metering options by using the menu. There you can select a few options. These include: evaluative, partial spot, evaluative, and central weighted average.

The term "evaluative" is usually the setting your camera has made as the default. It is a measurement of all the light that is in your frame. It's also smart to take an assessment of the object you're focusing on and then compensates for it. This means you'll take a good reading of of your surroundings (they might require a bit of adjustments in the post) while achieving a fantastic focus on the object in your focus.

The next step is partial. Partial metering is a method of measuring the region of light close to your focal point, but only that. This is great the case where your background doesn't have any significance while your subject does.

Spot metering functions similar to partial, but it uses only the focal point that is within the center of the viewfinder. You may also alter your focus point in case you wish to to determine a different part in the frame.

There is also a central weighted average. This is the option you likely don't need to utilize often. It diffuses light across the entire frame and focuses in centrality of frame. I think this is a good thing for subjects that are situated in the center of the frame, since it doesn't take into account your focus on the center of your frame.

Focus modes are available via the small button located on the left side of your keypad marked AF. There are three options that are labeled as the one-shot, AI Focus, and AI Servo. These are known by distinct names on Nikon as well as other brands of cameras however they all have similar functions.

One shot performs exactly as it's named after It focuses on a single shot. It will not focus until you take you finger off the shutter to concentrate another shot. This is useful for shooting photos, where you need to allow the model enough time to pose.

AI Servo is good for occasions, or maybe documentary photography in which you have the subject moving. Of course, you must determine the shutter speed in accordance with and this mode can capture continuous images and keep the subject in sharp focus and clearly defined.

The third option fourth is AI Focus, which uses both to make sure you get exactly what you want. In the event that the focus's depth or the distance to the focal point changes or farther away, it'll take an instant to adjust the distance depending

on the needs.

Chapter 11: Making the Action Shots

Motion captured in motion can result in fascinating and captivating photos. The process of capturing action isn't easy but the duration of the event is very short. This is why those rare photos are even more precious. It takes lots of patience and time to help a photographer develop reflexive skills that will enable him to record those moments.

To capture action photos You could consider investing in an appropriate tripod. Simple movements of pushing the shutter release button on your camera causes motion. This isn't ideal when you want to take pictures of the movement. Your camera must remain stable.

If you don't have an existing tripod then you may be able to locate tables or posts that you can rest your arms on. Monopods are also affordable that can be swung around railings, instead of carrying around a tripod that is heavy. Another method is to place the camera up on a level surface, and then set the timer for two seconds. The shutter release button is pressed and take your hands off as your camera captures the image without shaking your hands.

Certain cameras also come with image stabilization features that alert you to any camera shake that isn't intended.

When you set your camera for an extremely slow shutter speed, you'll be able to capture movements of objects that are captured by blur. For example, a photo of an animal flapping its wings will display blurred wings moving. This could make for a more exciting photograph than the bird perched on a tree.

It is the same technique employed when photographing water moving like fountains or waterfalls. The photos will display the mist effect, which resembles the water's rushing.

However If you wish to capture a particular moment of action, without blurring effect make sure you set your camera to the speed of shuttering at a high speed. This is a great method to employ when taking pictures of sporting events. The ability to capture a volleyball player the moment she hits the ball or watching an athlete in mid-tumble can make for interesting photos.

Also, remove your camera off of the tripod and observe the action. For instance, when you are shooting a moving vehicle you can pan your camera in the direction the car will create a blurred background, with an uncluttered automobile in the background. However, the rapid shutter could result in dim images and you should alter your ISO to make them appear brighter.

The majority of cameras come with the ability to burst, which allows the camera to take multiple photos quickly. Therefore, you are able to pick the one that best is from a variety of photos. The issue with the burst feature is that it could not give enough time for the camera to be focused on the subject. This can result in a variety of photographs that aren't in focus. It is better to shoot single, well-focused photos.

The latest models of cameras include a sports mode which automatically prepares your camera to capture action. This is a great feature to use if you are interested the idea, but in different circumstances and conditions it is better off using manually controlled controls.

In action photography, you need to learn to anticipate the movements that your subject is making. The crowd at a sporting event is likely to applaud, stand, and wave when their team scores the crucial move. Be prepared for this moment and try to keep it in your memory.

When photographing cheerleaders, be sure to take pictures of the best formations and stunts but not when they're performing floor work. It's likely to be a regret that you finish making a snap too early or late, since the time may not be there ever again.

Another method to learn is to prepare. This means you set your camera that you anticipate that the object to appear. A child who is playing on the bottom of a slide will be on the bottom of the slide. So, place your camera in the bottom of the slide and capture precisely the moment the subject enters frame. You'll find that you get a better chance of having a sharp picture when you do this.

For compact cameras and SLRs, you can focus the camera prior to taking a shot by pressing the shutter release half-way before pressing it fully to shoot. The cameras on touch phones let you first press the area you would like the camera to concentrate.

It is therefore crucial to know the best place to put yourself. Make sure you are in the middle of the action, or at the very least, be in the front of it. Cheap seats aren't enough for you if you're looking to capture the best photos. Many events, such as plays, sports or even shows will not permit you to photograph in the front, where the photographers paid.

Choose to go to informal events that will not be hesitant to take some photos to add to your collection. Be aware of the lighting and background.

For concert photography it's not good if the majority of your pictures are obstructed by equipment that block the view of the primary image. If you are in a location that has lights constantly blazing through your lens could be frustrating. Also, be aware of what could occur as you shoot your photographs.

The use of your flash can be beneficial when trying to draw attention to a subject, while leave the background in a blur. However, the majority of cameras with compact bodies come with flashes that can only be used at only a short distance. They're most useful when you're close to the subject or in dim lighting conditions.

Frame your photo well. If you're taking pictures of skateboarders jumping off staircases Don't simply take a picture that shows the skateboarder. Include in the shot the skateboard on which he is riding and also a part of the staircase. If the area is fascinating, include in the photo the surrounding buildings or behind them covered in colorful graffiti. This can tell an entire story rather than just an individual boy leaping in the air.

Also, when you take photos of moving animals or people ensure that the faces are clean. It's always fascinating to observe the effort sportsmen put into their sport when they smile or tighten their muscles when taking a picture.

Chapter 12: How to Set Up your DSLR's Flash for your DSLR

DSLR cameras could be confusing for novices because they offer a variety of choices. If you have a point-and shoot camera, you have only two choices: (a) use flash or (b) do not use flash. When you own DSLRs, there are many options to choose from. DSLR there are a number of ways to use flash that can be selected from. You can elevate your photography to a new height using these flashes however only if you are aware of what they are and how to utilize them.

Auto TTL

Through the Lens (TTL) is the auto-flash mode. The flash comes with various strengths, and the camera decides which one to use.

Red-Eye Reduction

Eyes that look red in photos are gone. It is no longer necessary to be concerned about the appearance of red eyes in photographs and, with the help of a DSLR you can ensure that there aren't any eyes that are red, so you do not need to fix them later on in Photoshop. The Red-Eye Reduction feature uses multiple flashes to constrict the pupils while taking photos and drastically reduces the possibility of seeing the appearance of a red eye.

Fill Flash

Another issue for cameras is great images are damaged in the event that sunlight is in the background and you must adjust the shadows later in order to let the photo appear crystal clear. Fill Flash is a Fill Flash option is used to make flash happen even when the camera doesn't recognize the necessity to use it. It can be utilized outdoors to capture photos, to stop sunlight from creating harsh shadows on your face or inside to reduce the light that enters through glass doors and windows.

Slow Sync

To enhance the brightness of the backgrounds while taking photographs, use the slow Sync mode. It reduces the speed of shutter and boosts how much light is reflected.

High Speed Sync

This is a popular option for photographers who are using external flashes in conjunction with their cameras. In this mode the shutter speed will increase to allow for photos of sports or action. This is also useful to take pictures in bright sunlight, or when it is necessary to use a fast shutter.

Rear Curtain

If you choose to use the rear Curtain mode the camera will hold off the use of flash. It will be activated just before the exposure is over.

Flashes that repeat

This mode utilizes flash multiple times. The camera splits flash into discrete flashes to allow photos to be taken throughout the duration that the shutter is open.

Wireless Mode

This is the mode to use in conjunction with an external flash. It syncs off-camera flash with your DSLR to allow you to remotely start the flash.

Manual Mode

As you've already guessed that the flash can be used in different ways. Each mode is designed to make use of flash in a particular manner. The manual mode is intended for advanced users, and provides them with greater control. You can set up the flash using this mode to regulate the intensity. Once you've mastered the fundamentals of flash, play using the manual mode to discover how your pictures will be affected by the mode.

Chapter 13: Working with Perspective and Depth

We've now gone over the fundamentals in photographing (choice of camera and exposure, as well as composition) let's look at methods you can begin taking incredible photos, right from the start.

Perspective and Depth

Exploring depth and perspective is among the initial subsequent steps that people do when they begin to make interesting pictures. It means they use the natural properties of how far from an object is and contrast it with the largest part of the image. This is commonly referred to as The

Three Layers (foreground, background, and mid-ground).

Tips: Visualize images that are a mix of these layers. Take a look out the window. What is the most intriguing thing that your attention is attracted to? Is it something near (on the window's edge?) or is it a building that is in the distance? Perhaps something in between? By shifting the focus of your image, to highlight the various elements, you can alter the entire image!

Three Layers. Three Layers.

Foreground = the 'Closest' part of the image, proximity to the camera. It is typically towards the bottom and the front of the photo (although there are occasions when it could be a tree's branches hanging over the picture from above, which is closer to the ground!)

The mid-ground is usually an important element in the photograph, and includes the buildings, landscape, and other things you wish to take a picture of. Great for landscape or nature photography.

Background = Farthest from the camera. Usually blurry and considered to be the 'moodpiece' in the image.

Snap a photo of an individual in their natural setting. If you are at the background, it conveys an immediate "I am here" with details of their face and emotions at the time.

If you put the person in the middle of the scene, it looks a bit like a picture from a school. They are part of a larger picture.

If you take the same element - the individual and put them in the background suddenly, they appear to be in a different place and wandering, even though they're in exactly the same pose and position that they did in the background! When you play around with these layers and elements you can create stunning images.

Consider:

* What's the background? What kind of mood is it setting for the artwork? Are you in a dark mood? Are you seeing a stormy sky or a sunny, summery one?

* Which element is most intriguing and makes the main subject of the picture all-encompassing? Are you looking at

something close-up such as a flower or faces or distant like the spire of a church?

Diminishing

One of the most important aspects of perspective is that of decreasing. It is a common feature in photographs in some degree or not. The trick is to find the horizon point.

The line of the horizon is quite obvious it is the point at which the sky meets the ground or where the ocean connects with the sky. It's also the farthest location in your photo. In the case of miniatures and close-ups This is the area where your photo disappears in the distance.

The horizon line is the most distant point on the photo which is the point at which you lose all perception of perspective. The horizon lines become one and all details are lost. From this hazy, unobserved area, the rest of the image'stands out and then moves towards the viewer in increasing and clearer clarity.

This Diminishing refers the act of the image becoming smaller and more fuzzy. But, it can also work in the opposite direction, as when the image gets too large for the eye to see, and the image becomes blurred. This is how depth perception operates and how you focus your attention on an elements in the middle of the ground, but all around , it's fuzzy!

Tips:

Explore how your objects relate to the diminution point. By putting your subject or the intriguing feature further into the decreasing horizon the subject becomes less attractive. This can be used to create a contrast with other elements of your image such as fading Bumblebees flying away next to a flower in the foreground?

Or, the reverse A foreground close-up of a

bumblebee   soaring   towards   an

encroaching, distant field of flowers?

Chapter 14: The Expert Tips to Guide You Through as a Beginner

Here are some professional tips you could apply to speed up your way towards becoming a professional photographer.

1. If you want your photo to remain breathtaking and beautiful, always use RAW.

RAW is a type of file format for images that is that is similar to JPEG. RAW is the preferred format due to the fact that it permits the photographer to determine what the image should look after post-processing.

A Quick Tip: DSLRs take photos in RAW format by default.

2. Make use of a tripod when the situation requires it.

A tripod does not render you less of an artist, except if you're using it with no justifiable reason. In some instances, you could come across a photograph-worthy situation where the subject is in motion and the use of a speedy shutter isn't an alternative. In such a case you may want to utilize an tripod instead of hands. The tripod is not just able to ensure that the camera is steady and steady, but assist you in coming up with photos that are level even when you're on uneven ground. This is accomplished by using the spirit or bubble levels included with the tripod.

3. Focus manually.

It is important to remember that the most effective way to get used to how to focus is to work it out by hand. Your camera does not know what it should be focusing on. You're just telling it to concentrate.

You can turn off the camera's auto focal (AF) after which select the locations on which you'd like to focus. You can also utilize the camera's focal lock feature. This feature will assist you in creating a narrow DOF.

4. Check out the eyes of your subject.

When you are a novice it is likely that you'll practice often with portraits. Keep in mind that instinctively people are drawn by the eyes of the subject. So, it's normal for photographers to concentrate on their subject's eyes while the portrait is being shot.

5. Buy a good lens.

If you are a beginner is recommended that you switch to using a prime lens when you have the first digital camera. Primarily, prime lenses do not come with a zoom feature but it requires to use all of the crucial elements, and that is a good way to get used to.

Prime lenses aren't so expensive as you believe it to be. A prime lens of 50mm will cost around $150, or less.

6. Use the stabilize function if it is in use.

Some lenses include the ability to stabilize images. If the lens you have is equipped with this you can turn it on whenever you're trying to take pictures using a small aperture and a slow shutter speed. Be sure to switch it off when you've got a tripod you want to use, as it could negatively impact the final outcome of your photograph.

7. Less ISO is better.

Don't let this mislead you. If I say that less ISO is better it means that you will get better quality photographs. Make sure to make sure you set the ISO in the range of normal. This will ensure more crisp, clearer and sharper images, unless you are looking to eliminate unwelcome digital noise.

8. The sharpest isn't the broadest.

They say that having too many or too little of anything is harmful. This is also true for aperture. It is advised to make sure that you set it to the aperture of f/8.

A shutter speed of f/8 gives you not a wide nor deep DOF. It will give you just enough DOF to concentrate on your subject and create sharper images.

9. It's not always trendy to be flashy.

Flash accessories can assist you create stunning images in the event that you are able to make the most of them.

If there's no other method to ensure a high-quality lighting, then you can put the flash on top of your camera (as described in the prior chapters). Place it in a position that the flash is in contact with the lens's pane. Additionally, ensure to bounce it off of the ceiling or wall to ensure that it creates the naturally lit effect.

10. Always remember, speed matters.

If you want to get sharpness and prevent motion blurring Your shutter speed needs to be set to a fraction of your focal length of the lens. For instance, a 30- millimeter lens requires 1/30 of an second shutter speed.

If it gets difficult to hold the camera in steady hands, it's not a sin to activate the burst mode on your DSLR. The burst mode permits users to select from a variety of pictures. Of course, you have to select one that does not show signs of you using the camera in a shaken hand.

Chapter 15: Metering

Photographers need to know how much light available and if it is enough light available to create an accurate picture of what your eyes can see. We would like to believe that we're able to determine this without any equipment however, when you've snapped a photo only to find an unnatural exposure due to inadequate lighting, we are aware that assistance is required.

Your camera comes with built-in settings to measure light. It calculates so that you do not need to worry about it.

Terminology

Metering is the measurement of the luminosity of the target.

Metering sensor: Automatically determines the luminosity of your subject.

Evaluative metering is ideal for portraits as well as evenly backlit subjects that are evenly backlit. Cameras with this feature will use this setting automatically to achieve the correct exposure.

Partial metering is a good choice to brighter backgrounds. The metering rate is around 9 percent from the camera's viewfinder.

Spot metering is best to measure a particular part of a scene or subject like 3.8 percent of the subject's viewfinder.

Center-weighted metering: evaluates the central point of the subject. It afterwards averages light across every scene.

White-balance is the way that the camera is able to deliver the correct color.

Manual Mode

You can give your camera with the task of determining what amount of light that the exposure is receiving when you are in manual mode. You can do this by setting your shutter speed, ISO and aperture. By experimenting with all of the modes previously used and understanding the distinctions will assist you in improving your photography.

Once you're ready, you can select manual mode to adjust the measurement.

You'll need to look at the scene as your camera to become higher at the meters aspect of photography.

One suggestion is to consider gray. If you view the subject and think that gray is the only color that you can think of, it will assist you. It will be as the camera you are. The camera's metering mechanism examines the image you'd like to capture and then returns settings for aperture and shutter speed according to the information it receives. This is referred to as middle gray, because you are able to alter the settings to lighten or increase the brightness of the overall picture.

An effective way to comprehend the concept of metering is to use white, black, or gray objects.

In a book of the year the young girl with long blonde locks and white shirts could have appeared pale and downright white with just her blue eyes shining. The photographer, however, was aware of the concept of light and measuring. The model appeared to be three-dimensional with her skin showing tan and her eyes being a stunning blue, set against her blonde hair and the white in her shirt.

If you don't have metering built into your camera, or are using the wrong setting, the black subject will appear grey, while a white one will only appear at the darkest areas and gray appears white.

Try it. Set three subjects which include white, black, and gray. After that three subjects, snap a picture of each one and observe what happens. If the objects are photographed in isolation, you will see the strange shades.

Then, set the 3 subjects to the camera. Snap a picture. The camera's metering mechanism analyzes the three colors, and then provides middle gray. This means that you get black and that the gray color is grey as well as white. Your camera set to automatic will always display middle gray. If there is a contrast the colors may be off.

We all know that there are more colours than white, black and gray. This means that your photos need to have more than the middle gray in order for the metering process to function correctly.

Let's look at the contrast between the moon against a dark sky. You walk outside and you don't see any lighting. The moon is at its full. The camera is able to see the glowing light and the black sky. Instead of seeing the moon turn yellow, as you can see the image you take will be black-and-white with no definition of the moon. It's nothing more than a bright object.

With the right measurement the shutter speed, aperture along with ISO you can identify the colors that the naked eye perceives and then capture these colors on your camera. The first step is to learn how to discern the light that is available, and what to do with it contemplating middle gray.

In the discussion of ISO in chapter 2 evaluative spots, partial center-weighted, and spot were they were mentioned. There are a few DSLRs come with these features. However, if you discover that your camera has, you could make adjustments to your metering settings in manual mode to take into account the "gray" the camera is seeing.

It is possible to instruct your camera to concentrate on 100 percent 99%, 100 percent, 3.8% or the center of the subject to measure in manually mode (depending upon the model of camera that you are using). If you want to alter the white balance by using spots, evaluative, partial or center-weighted settings you can choose the mode your preference is based on the common subject matter.

White balance is an essential indicator for the metering process. If you are able to detect the white balance in your camera, and offset by other colors, it can assist your camera in figuring out what the color needs to be.

The hue of light depends on a variety of factors, such as how much light there is in the scene, the time of the morning, how the day is and whether you're shooting in the shade or light. Flash, when used in the scene, can be used like sunlight and in bringing colors to your image which otherwise would be obscuring.

To aid the camera's metering mechanism, you'll need to know how white balance . You must make white, and white under lighting. If you see off-white or gray it is likely that there is something wrong with the light you're seeing. This is the reason you find photographers with equipment to balance the light. White balancing and shades can be used to aid in reading the meter more accurately than white, black and middle grey.

Have you ever snapped a photo in dim light and noticed that it was washed out? The color was not as vibrant as you expected, maybe the it appeared yellower than green? The reason is all to be related to white balance and the metering. For Canon Four meters are available in the WB setting for white balance. You can alter the settings to increase the brightness according to the light you observe.

It's always an excellent idea that you test the camera using the default setting and then switch to the other three options that are available for white balance in order to find the one that provides the closest color that your naked eye can see.

Picture Example #8: Rainbows

Have you ever witnessed the rainbow and wondered if the rainbow could be captured? Perhaps, you tried to determine the color of the sky but it didn't appear? It is all to have to do in the white balance, metering and white of the camera.

To make a photo of a rainbow it is necessary to have three elements. It is necessary to have an actual rainbow and a white cloud in the location, and a contrast hue, like blue sky. If you're having gray skies because of an occurrence of storm, the rainbow will vanish, and you'll get an unlit sky and a gray cloud.

But, with the metering adjustments that allow you to select various white balance settings, you can enhance the colors of the rainbow by using lighting. When you next observe a rainbow, test it. It is possible that you will get something similar to this

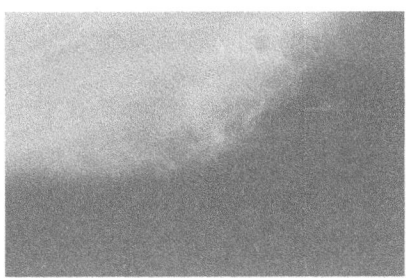

It is possible to see the rainbow in the yellow, blue light red, white cloud. The photo was captured using the auto setting, so you can imagine what would happen if the photographer tried to alter the metering setting to reveal brighter colors of rainbow in the white sky with blue clouds. The blue might be more sharp as could color of the rainbow. The cloud could have looked as white as well, had the photographer adjusted to get the best image.

Summarising Metering

Metering allows you to read the light. The white balance can help to improve the contrast in the color of the subject, ensuring that the image is as vivid that it seems to the untrained eye. If you switch the white balance and metering mode and white balance mode, you can make the colors more sharp, whereas dulling the colors, or seeing green instead of yellow and grey instead of black or gray in white.

Conclusion

The photos you create and edit using Photoshop can be breathtakingly gorgeous. We've shown you a variety of ways to create your photos, and there are several more options that you could consider trying. Portraits of singles and groups require different types of composition. You also can choose the classics to choose from for the classic families or couples looking for a unique photograph to commemorate a significant event within their own lives.

Utilizing the techniques of light we have presented to you, and by adjusting your camera to match the lighting available it is possible to create stunning images. Make sure to save the images in RAW format as JPG. Format is always compressed and it isn't as good before the image is loaded into your program. Adjust your camera, and then get used to the various adjustments available to allow you to create the most stunning images you've ever taken. When you begin to experiment and become comfortable with the photos you're taking you'll find that they are second-nature. But, if it is helpful to you to improve your photography make sure to keep notes on the settings you tried because it will assist you learn.

If you notice that you're constantly needing to compensate for poor lighting, overexposure or under exposure using Photoshop this is an excellent indication that you must be more attentive to the settings of your camera in order to improve photos. Explore different settings, and test the ISO since it makes an impact.

Once you have your images ready you can begin to work on them using Photoshop Bridge because you'll can access your photos and the process gets much more easy when you use this feature as component of your Photoshop experience. There are many ways to improve the photos you do with the camera, and a myriad of factors can be a factor. If you glance through the viewfinder, maybe you didn't notice a speck of light that's in the wrong spot or hair that is off the mark. Photoshop can make your photos perfect and that's the goal of this tutorial is about - taking photos and enhancing them to ensure that your portraiture is improved and your appearance is flawless.

Try out the various tools available in Photoshop and gradually become familiar with them as there are various methods of manipulating images, which they believe will yields the most effective outcomes. These are the strategies that I have found to be the most efficient and can be very efficient but every photographer knows what they wish to achieve with specific images.

The book covers an extensive amount of ground since portrait photography is an enormous topic. There are a myriad of variations and plenty you can do with your photos to make them better. While many people are enthralled by tools for cropping, you should avoid it if possible , as you risk lose precious pixels, at the very least until you are aware of the best way to avoid it! In the meantime, ensure that your composition is perfect and capture photos while being aware that perfection begins in the photo stage and should not be achieved through cropping images in a way that isn't necessary.

Once you've finished reading the book, do the various exercises and find out more about the settings for light on your camera as well as the various F/stops. Learn about the proper exposure as well as the right ISO. This all contributes to your portraits getting better and more appealing. Utilizing Photoshop you are able to experiment with softening and enhancing images as well as adjust those areas that pose a problem. A photo that has been taken with the correct settings can be improved with the help of Photoshop to polish the picture to the highest quality.